D0121082

101 THINGS TO DO WITH A DULL CHURCH

101 Things To Do With a Dull Church

The Complete Guide for the Bored Again Christian

MARTIN WROE & ADRIAN REITH

Illustrated by Simon Jenkins
Special thanks to Simon Parke

MINSTREL
Eastbourne

Copyright © Martin Wroe & Adrian Reith 1989

First published 1989

All rights reserved.
No part of this publication may be reproduced or
transmitted in any form or by any means, electronic
or mechanical, including photocopy, recording, or any
information storage and retrieval system, without
permission in writing from the publisher.

Front cover design by Simon Jenkins

British Library Cataloguing in Publication Data

Wroe, Martin
  101 things to do with a dull church.
  I. Title II. Reith, Adrian
  828'.91409

  ISBN 1-85424-063-3 (Minstrel)
        0-7324-0435-5 (Albatross)

Copublished in Australia by Albatross Books
PO Box 320, Sutherland, NSW 2232

Printed in Great Britain for
Minstrel, an imprint of Monarch Publications Ltd
1 St Anne's Road, Eastbourne, E Sussex BN21 3UN by
Richard Clay Ltd, Bungay, Suffolk
Typeset by Nuprint Ltd, Harpenden, AL5 4SE.

For
Rev Brian Wroe
and
Rev Ivor Reith

Two not very dull churchmen

CONTENTS

Introduction

101 Things To Do With a Dull Church

...it's what a lively church is all about. Probably.

If you've ever sat in a church service and wondered what was going on and why—don't worry, you are not alone—this book is for you.

This book is for you if the thought of going to church on Sunday morning does not always make you leap out of bed.

It is for you if—like us—when you do get to church you sometimes wish you hadn't leapt out of bed.

Still, we are not alone. Jesus must have felt the same way, sometimes.

Being involved in church can be exciting.

This is for the odd occasion when it isn't.

1

Drastic Action

Phhhnntt!

1. Drastic action: on the building

(a) Have it demolished. Write to a local demolition firm saying that the building has been compulsorily purchased to make way for a new motorway and the building needs to be flattened within a week.

(b) Blow it up. Call the police, tell them you have received a tip-off that there is a bomb in the church. They will send in the bomb disposal squad who will mistake the Deathwatch Beetle ticking for a time-bomb and blow up the church for you with a convenient controlled explosion.

(c) Conceal a brick a week under your Bible as you leave the church — for the rest of your life. (Difficult with stone or concrete constructions.)

(d) March around the building every day for a week blowing a bugle borrowed from the scouts. On the last day shout a lot.

(e) Order it to be cast into the sea (on the faith-as-a-grain-of-mustard-seed principle).

2. Drastic action: on the members

Wake them up with:
(a) Smelling salts concealed in hymn book (suggest 'Thine be the Glory').
(b) Fire a starting pistol.
(c) Announce the last hymn.
(d) Whoopee prayer cushions.
(e) Smoke alarms—most effective in 'high' churches.

3. Drastic action: on the vicar/minister/pastor/deacon/bishop

(a) Start sending her/him the appointments pages of the relevant church newspaper with likely posts helpfully ringed in red.
(b) Whenever you see him/her emphasise how their predecessor was taken away mysteriously by men in white coats after being in the church about the same amount of time.
(c) Make regular phone calls in a deep gruff voice intoning the words, 'The Lord says, "Time to go, my servant."'
(d) Break into the Vicarage/Manse one night and write high up on the wall MENE, MENE, TEKEL, UPARSIN (meaning 'You have been weighed in the balance and found wanting', Daniel 5:25).
(e) Get one of your members with the gift of prophecy to proclaim loudly in the packed Sunday morning service that the Lord is calling your minister to 'higher things'—in Outer Mongolia.

The pastor's call came out of the blue…

2

Services For All Occasions

It's funny, but lots of people when they think of 'church' merely think of attending the odd service. And let's face it, most church services *are* odd. But there is much more to any church than mere services. But—who cares?—why not begin with services anyway?

Not everyone likes a formal style of service that is written down.

Some churches prefer to demonstrate their freedom by doing exactly the same thing each week—from memory. That's why we've included a variety of styles below.

Some people say their church does not have a style. We say phooey.

We have written a number of new services that you may not yet be using in your own church but which could make it more interesting. Use this approach to write your own services.

4. Order of service for a harvest festival in the city where nothing ever grows

After the bedlam subsides a bit, the president may say these words:

Minister: We are gathered here on this fine sunny day to celebrate the wonderful provision of food on our tables. Blessed be the fish finger, the cheeseburger, the prawn flavoured crisp, the diet cola which containeth nigh unto one calorie.

Let us begin our service with hymn number 103 in the blue book 'We plough the field with tractors'.

After this frightful hymn has been sung, the minister may turn to the choirmaster or organist and say:

Remind me not to have that dreadful hymn again next year.

All: Amen.

Minister: Let us now bring our harvest gifts up to the rail to be distributed among the poor, needy and clergy. Please remember that we do not accept anything whatsoever containing artificial colouring, additives, neither perishable goods, nor eggs, sweaty things that are wrapped in clingfilm, nor anything cheap and nasty.

If you want to make a credit card donation slide your card in the slot provided in the rail and key in the amount. Your account will be debited.

Have a nice day.

All: Amen.

Minister: Our final hymn is 'Only the crumbliest, flakiest chocolate tastes like chocolate never tasted before' on the overhead projector, omitting verses 3 and 4.

5. Service of blessing for animals just in case they don't go to heaven after all

When all the animals have been safely herded into the church building and are quietly seated in the pews (this may take some time) the service may begin.

Parson: Lo.
Cows: Moo moo.
Parson: The cattle are lowing.
Carol Singer: The baby awakes.
Geese: Hiss.
Parson: In the words of St James of Herriott: 'Blessed are the lovely little kittens, the loyal doggie, the noble horse, the wise owl, the happy budgie, the clever dolphin, the big, big, big whale.'
Animals: You bet.

It was during the second hymn that the animals first noticed…

Parson:	Blessed are the sly fox, the cheeky monkey, the pungent skunk, the pointed porcupine, the oh-so-hungry vulture, the ripping, slicing, chomping shark—the Arnold Schwarzenegger of the ocean—the mouse and the moose, the pussy and the python, the officer and the gentleman, er…and those funny Australian things that crawl upside down…for they shall inherit a lot more than those nasty people that complain about the dogs' mess on the pavement.
Vet:	That's quite enough.
All:	And also with moo.

Note: *At close of service care should be taken to wipe the collection off the seats.*

6. Baptism service for children who are too young to know what is happening

Minister:	Who bringeth this horrible little specimen for dunking?
Parents:	I suppose we do.
Child:	Waaaaaaaaaaaaaaa!
Father: *(If there be one)*	Belt up or I'll…
Minister:	Ahem. Wassisnameagain?
Mother:	Excuse me your Highness, where's the photographer?
Font:	(SPLASH)
Child:	Waaaaaaaaaaaaaaaaa!

'Let's have those vows once more—and this time
as if you really mean it.'

All: And also with you.

Father: *(If there be only one)* So that's it then, Vicar?

Minister: S'pose it is. Amen.

Parents: Right then. See you at his wedding, then.

All: And also with you.

7. Marriage before God of two people who don't believe in God

The organist may begin by playing a tune by Lennon and McCartney like 'All you need is love'. When the happy couple is at the front of the church the service shall begin with these words:

Minister: Excuse me, what did you say your names were?

Bride: Boo hoo!

Groom: Gavin and Sandra.

Minister: Dearly beloved, we are gathered together in the presence of Almighty God to witness the marriage of Gary and Selina who I've not seen before and doubtless won't see again.

Caterer: *Three* hundred guests?!

Minister: I can't see why they want to get married in church because they don't believe in God—but we'll carry on with the charade regardless—because it's fun to dress up and it wouldn't quite be the same in a Registry Office now would it?

If there is any congregation left, he may continue:

Photographer: Let's get this over with and sing the song on your sheet: 'She loves you, yeah, yeah, yeah.' Can you hold it there? (WHIRR...CLICK... FLASH)

After this abomination comes the marriage ceremony:

Minister: You've been living together now for four years—so now I pronounce you man and wife. Thank you and goodnight.

Photographer: Just one more. (FLASH... BANG.) Lovely.

At the exchanging of the rings the Minister may say, 'Er...can I have my cheque now, please?'

All: Cooee—this way. I just want to take a photo. Amen.

Video Director: Sorry, held up in traffic, can we just run through the service again from the top?

Caterer: *Five* hundred guests is it now?!

8. A short service of blessing for those approaching baldness

Priest: The Lord be with you.
People: Thank you.
Priest: For your hair won't be for much longer.
Communal lament of the people:

> Where are you, O Lord, as my hair disappears, as each shampoo leaves more of my precious thatch clinging to the side of the bath? People say, 'Hello Shiny Top,' and I say, 'Where is my God?' People say, 'I've seen more hair on a snooker ball,' and I say again, 'Where is my God?'
>
> Yet even though my head increasingly resembles that of Frank Bough, yet will I not lose hope. For I mean he's not poor is he? And perhaps I shall live to present *The Travel Programme* yet.

Suggested reading: 2 Samuel 18:1–18.
(This narrative records the death of Absalom after he catches his hair in the branches of a tree—thus revealing some of the biblical advantages of hair loss.)

A time of confession may follow, after which the priest, if he feels like a wind-up, may say:

Priest: Now go—and thin no more.

Suggested final song: 'Be bald, be bald, for the Lord your God is with you.' *(Taken from the original version of this popular song:* 'Be Bold, be bold,' *etc. This slight amendment makes for a moving affirmation of baldness before departure.)*

Many people, of course, write their own services—adapting to the special needs of the local congregation. Use this list to write your own modern church services.

9. Service of fumigation for lady with cats two rows from the back who stinks to high heaven

10. Service of confirmation for teenagers who are just doing it because their dad said they had to

11. Service of explanation for people who have just endured the 1662 prayer book service

12. Midnight mass for people weaving their way back from the pub at closing time

13. Service of Christian divorce for people who wished they hadn't been in the service of holy matrimony

14. Toy service for local children's home to receive headless action men and incomplete jigsaws

15. Service of apology to congregation after preacher has preached another dull sermon

16. Commissioning service for a missionary leaving for somewhere where mobile phones don't work

17. Marriage service in the presence of congregation of divorced persons

18. Mission service (a) for the converted; (b) for the unconverted

19. Funeral service—for someone you didn't know from Adam

20. Service of holy communion (except with certain women bishops)

21. Service on outbreak of armed hostilities with a dirty rotten foreign power

3

Prayers, Thanksgivings And Supplications

What *is* prayer? Talking with God. Amazing really—how come in so many churches the prayers are so boring?

Note: No special form of words is required in order to pray. However, some people do find a written prayer focuses the attention. We have tried to include a number of different prayer styles and several common topics.

The curious thing about prayer is that public prayers often tend to be long and wordy while private prayers tend to be very short and to the point—especially if you are in trouble. Funny that.

Use this list of Prayers, Thanksgivings and Supplications to give you ideas for prayer.

The committal of the lost credit cards…

22. Prayer on the loss or mislaying of a filofax

Oh Lord, why on earth didn't I make a photocopy of my address book as I always intended to? Verily, I am a stupid twit.

I mean this most sincerely—if I find that missing filofax—I swear that I will cut back on expensive meals out and give a generous donation to Tear Fund.

23a. Praise on finding a clean public lavatory that works

Abbreviated version: Phew!

23b. Lament on finding a dirty one that doesn't

Abbreviated version: Poo!

24. Thanksgiving on survival of black ski run

Help! This is *much* steeper than it looked! Please God, just get me down alive...I'll even do door-to-door evangelism...Oh, Mummy!

('Amen' not required when in mortal danger.)

25. Prayer of thanks for not getting caught speeding

That was close. I won't go over the speed limit ever again. Well, not until that police car is out of sight.

Amen.

26. A prayer of hope for the soul of the chalet girl

(Particularly hoping she hasn't got a large boyfriend.)

27. A prayer to find a husband/wife/both

This is probably one of the most fervently and frequently prayed prayers of all.

Version for women: Oh, oh, oh, oh, oh, oh, oh, oh, Lord. You said yourself that it isn't good for a man to be alone. So presumably it isn't good for this woman to be alone either. Why not solve two problems in one go by putting a gorgeous single hunk somewhere within striking distance of me, your frustrated servant? Together we will go anywhere in your service...honest...anywhere.

I take back what I said last time I prayed about this. I didn't mean to say that me being single was grossly unfair of you. I know I've got loads to be thankful for...um...er...well there's the...um...there's my record collection...my health...what else is there...a filofax that I never use...I'd willingly swap all those for *him*, whoever he is.

Er...except that last guy Cyril—couldn't have been *him* could it? Oh, no! He's a creep! Please God let it not be poor old Cyril—maybe I'd rather be a single missionary than face that.

Maybe I *should* become a missionary. California perhaps?

Amen.

28. A short prayer for the poor

Oh dear...amen.

29. Collect on the occasion of the preacher being over-impressed with himself

Lord, look kindly on this present congregation, and may the mighty wind of your Spirit blow where it will. But may it blow *particularly* venemously around the sermon notes of this flash Greaseball, thus scattering them in many and various ways around the church, and leaving him—if it be your will of course—with no option but to belt up.

It is the opinion of the elect here gathered, Father, that the keynote of the episode should be humiliation. His.

Amen.

PS: And thine be the glory, of course.

30. Collect on the occasion of hardly anyone turning up

Father, Son and Holy Spirit—we rejoice in your presence with us here tonight, for, if nothing else, you have more than doubled the numbers. Even if the collection is not going to be greatly affected.

Amen.

31. Prayer for the late to work

O Lord, thou knowest that I must be late for work today, due to the alcohol 'pressed down and running over' last night after the darts victory.

Let it be therefore that my boss is also late, due to some points failure or whatever—lest he notice my lapse and give that jerk Bernard my desk.

Er...that's about it.

Amen.

PS: Sorry.

32. Prayer on the occasion of utter boredom in church

O Lord, this service is so dull that I think I must be dead. But if it be, Lord, by your grace and favour, that I am not in fact dead—merely stunned into mind-numbing oblivion by the overall tedium and general inconsequentiality of the proceedings—grant your servant this: grant that the Vicar becomes 'called up yonder'* to that 'place which you have prepared for him' right away...if that be not too forward a request, of course.

Amen.

*Note: For those whose theologies allow, 'raptured' may be substituted here.

33. Collect for the feast day of some really obscure saint

We gather today, O Lord, to celebrate the feast day of St _____ .

I say 'celebrate', but let's be honest Lord, the whole thing's about as festive as a funeral in February. The church is freezing, there's only four of us here, and we know nothing about the old bat anyway.

Well, it's true, isn't it? Just post-brandy monastery gossip, recorded by some poor monk in Latin millions of years ago, making even the Ark seem contemporary.

Frankly Lord, if this is a feast day, give us a fast day any day of the week.

Er...amen.

34. Thanksgiving that the Sunday newspaper isn't any heavier this week

35a. Thanksgiving that you do not face the choice the rich young ruler faced between following Jesus or keeping his wealth

35b. Prayer for help when you realise you *do* have that choice

'Lord...it's for you-hoo!'

36. Supplication for the prompt arrival of the words 'and finally' during the sermon

37. Prayer that the pastor will not try to tackle Darwin's Theory of Evolution during the sermon again

38. Prayer that the church secretary doesn't suggest another protest against Sunday trading outside W H Smith Do-It-All this afternoon

39. Supplication that minister doesn't invite congregation to 'greet one another with the peace—especially someone you have never met before'. (Complementary prayer that the person next to you doesn't have BO.)

40a. Short prayer of thanks for a parking space if you drive a Volvo Estate

40b. Even shorter version if you drive a Mini Metro

41a. Prayer of secret relief that God has not called you to be a Roman Catholic in Nicaragua, a Pentecostal in the USSR, a Protestant or Catholic in Ulster, anyone at all in Ethiopia or the Sudan

41b. A longer prayer of comfort and strength for those who are there anyway

Church
Improvements

42. The television option

If you are cheesed off with your church because there is nobody in the pew except you, why not:

Write immediately to the producers of *Songs of Praise*, the most popular religious programme on British television, and invite them to come to your own church this Sunday.

A televised church service, for some reason always packs in the crowds—lights, cameras, equipment, technicians and even some congregation. People will come from miles around—the pubs, the council estate, the bingo hall, the BBC—even the odd regular chuch-goer. All just to worship God. (All of a sudden.)

Note: if you manage to get a seat it is much more impressive to be filmed (for the millions of viewers) singing along lustily—with your hymnbook the right way up.

If you fail to get *Songs of Praise* to come to your

'And of course we have an overflow hall
next door—just in case.'

church, forge an invitation to your minister inviting him to take part in one a few miles away—then take the evening off to watch *The Antiques Road Show*.

43. In-service entertainment—the perfect pew

Pews are hard, slippery and generally uncomfortable, but there is no law—as far as we know—against designing your own. In fact in centuries past the wealthy, landed and noble would have them custom-made to fit their own bottoms. Nobody else could sit in their pews which were roped off when they were not there—like the Directors' Box at Chelsea.

You too can follow in this excellent tradition.

The perfect pew

DIVINE DRINKS' CABINET: including stay-fresh communion wine-box with choice of bread sticks, bread cubes or vacuum-packed wafers.

FLOOR-LEVEL LIGHTING: in keeping with 'Thy word shall be a lamp unto my feet'.

SACRED SOUND SYSTEM: to pump the music up to a decent volume.

TV/VIDEO UNIT: for watching more exciting services than the one you are in.

ECCLESIA-PHONE: a special mobile phone for calling your accountant when you are ready to 'sell everything and come follow me'.

RAPTURE RADAR: this will give you thirty seconds warning of an impending rapture. Ejector seat will automatically operate.

WARDROBE: in case you have to rush off to a party/disco/funeral/fancy-dress party/prison after the service.

SAUNA: to keep the 'Temple of the Holy Spirit' (ie your body) in trim.
FOOT MASSAGER: essential considering 'How beautiful on the mountains are the feet of him who brings good news.'

44. Robovicar: the preprogrammed, stand-in minister

Are you having trouble with your present minister/vicar/deacon/pastor? No problem when you plug in *Robovic* (or the non-conformist *Stand-in Min*). Take a look at the all-singing, all-dancing, all-purpose, all-powerful, all-in-one remote controlled artificially intelligent *Stand-in Min*—for when your preacher is having an off day or an off life.

Robovicar/the Stand-in Min features include:
HIP-HOP DANCE BUTTON: fantastic for the aerobics class and to offer ideas to the charismatic one-steppers.
BRAIN OF EINSTEIN: can engage in debate with scientists who believe that modern science has discredited the bible.
PRINCE CHARMING MODE: so that the old ladies still come along, bless 'em.
RHETORIC OF A HOT AIR BALLOON: to get the congregations airborne after years of pew-sleeping.
WISE CRACKING ONE-LINER PROGRAMME: funny, sharp, witty but non-sexist and environmentally right-on.
VOICE OF 1000-MEMBER WELSH MALE VOICE CHOIR: will get the goosebumps rising on the back of the neck and the congregation singing revival into the locality again.

45. Economy version—the Sony Walkmin

Not unlike the Sony Walkman but with interesting preachers in the headphones.

46. Ecclesia-plex—the multi-churchmanship church complex

Follow the trend that cinemas have successfully pioneeredrecently—*diversify.*

Offer a range of exciting church service options. In other words—just give 'em what they want.

SCREEN ONE: Traditional 'Hell fire and brimstone' offering, complete with Ian Paisley and rabid fundamentalist Protestants *whipping* the congregation with their own sinful ways, *slashing* them with their unworthiness, *terrifying* them with the threat of *damnation*, but offering them *forgiveness* and *peace* with the *Almighty* only if they *believe* in a *seven-day creation* and that Jonah was literally swallowed by a *real* giant fish and lived and it wasn't a mythical truth but a *true truth.*

One and a half hours—includes two-hour sermon. Emphasis on emphasis.

SCREEN TWO: Trad. insipid Anglican offering fit for anyone—because it doesn't disturb anyone. Dull hymn; vicar with a funny voice; terrible choir of three people who can't sing; nine different books to be juggled; ten degrees below zero, etc.

One hour—includes five-minute homily. Guaranteed no challenge.

SCREEN THREE: Trad. High Anglo-Catholic; bells and smells; led in theatrical fashion; chantedprayersthatyoucan'tunderstandbecausetheyrunall-

The after-church fellowship...

thewordstogether; 90 percent chance of transubstantiation during Communion; a touch gothic; very male; very polite; lots of costumes, etc.

One hour—includes forty-five-minute Communion.

SCREEN FOUR: Modern charismatic service—dancing; shouting; singing; repetition; repetition; prophecies; speaking in tongues; speaking in gobbledygook; no-speaking-at-all-without-headscarf-or-male-attribute.

Eight hours—includes ten-year sermon, fifteen words from the Lord, nineteen Graham Kendrick choruses, an OHP, and 'Majesty' sung 356 times continuously.

SCREEN FIVE: Futuristic Inclusive Service for Her (F.I.S.H.)—in which God is never referred to as he (because he...er...is not male), she (because she...er...is not female), or it...because (s)he is a person. However, in a bid to bury the four-thousand-year-old illusion that God is male, has a beard and insists on men having dominion over women—the FISH services are always led by women. Women preside over Communion. Of course only women attend—usually with spiky green hair, green wellies and green Citroen 2CVs outside with No Nukes stickers in the back window.

Very short—to accommodate the TV crews who have a news deadline, and prefer punchy 'sound bites'.

SCREEN SIX: The Night Club Service—this will be packed full of young people all wearing black 'gothic' clothes; electronic music—a version of 'acid house'—reclaimed for the Lord; unbelievably loud; everybody stands throughout the service and dances continuously; low lights; psychedelic images flashing everywhere; worried parents hammering on the doors outside; very hot; very unlike church; very alternative; whistles; shouts; no drugs or smoking, but you do wonder.

Two hours—sermon is an unknown concept.
SCREEN SEVEN: Political Rally—pioneered in North America. Minister confuses church with right-wing political party. Congregation confuse church service with Party Conference.

Sermon replaced by Party Political Broadcast. Service followed by heavy canvassing of the local area.
SCREEN EIGHT: Bingo Hall—Caller/Minister opens his Bible at random, closes his eyes and points his finger at a text which he calls out. If your text comes up, you will have a strong conviction. You shout, 'House (of the Lord),' and obey the instruction before the music stops.

Entrance by collection. Winner takes all.
SCREEN NINE: Changing of the Guards—ideal tourist attraction and valuable invisible earnings.

Useful tool for pre-evangelism—particularly with foreign tourists. No religion involved, but at least you've got them in the building.
SCREEN TEN: Cinema—always useful to have one nearby.

47. Body contact in the body of Christ: the hug

The Bible calls the church 'the body of Christ'— funny that—because in this body the limbs manage to avoid all physical contact. Traditionally anyway.

However, in recent years the hug has been making a bit of a comeback in some churches up and down

Deirdre favoured the Kamikaze Hug...

the land. Generally the new Christian huggers—out of practice obviously—aren't sure where to put their bodies during their new Christian hugging.

Not so in all churches. Some are getting liberated. And that can make a church less dull...particularly if you are an observer.

Well, there's nothing irreligious about a good hug, or even, dare we say it, a nice wet smacker. Quite in keeping with the Apostle Paul's teaching to 'greet one another with a holy kiss'.

Instead of sleeping in your next service, try spotting these hug styles:

(a) The 'Russian bear' hug

Like Russian bears, and almost as dangerous.

(b) The 'I'm an evangelical' hug

No body contact—arms encircle other 'brother' or 'sister' and touch without infringing personal space. Takes practice.

(c) The 'I'm charismatic' hug

Body contact everywhere except pelvis and face regions. Quite practical with practice.

(d) The 'I need a hug' hug

Watch these. One of these huggers is after more than mere Christian greetings. They may want affirmation, encouragement or even body contact. They may even try to tell you something about your future together. Can be tricky.

(e) The 'blimey, (s)he's going to hug me' hug

One party reluctant. Very dangerous, but sometimes can be spotted in advance. Best to simply run.

(f) The 'must we really go through with this hug business?' hug

Both parties reluctant, heads turned away in silent protest. Very English. Worth looking for.

48. Cooling down and chilling out

Calming down your church when it starts to overheat.

Not all churches suffer from cold buildings and cold congregations. Fortunately some churches have plenty of life in them—which can sometimes lead to the opposite problem—'meltdown'. This is when the ecclesiastical engine is running so fast and hot that overheating occurs.

(Liberal theologians long ago developed a now outmoded 'God is dead' theology but it was left to more pentecostally inclined brothers and sisters to develop a more noticeable 'God is deaf' theology.)

LOCATING THE VOLUME KNOB AND THERMOSTAT IN YOUR SERVICES:

(a) Fit the minister out with diving boots

(Everybody gets hot when they jump about too much.)

(b) Pop sleeping pills in the communion wine

The elders at the Maranatha Fellowship were developing the gift of crowd control...

(c) Organise a visit from the minister of a nearby non-charismatic church

(Don't bother if it's an *anti*-charismatic church as this will only result in the volume knob being turned up further—to convert him.)

(d) Organise a full night of prayer and fasting for local revival before the Sunday service.

(e) (If congregation are still raving and dancing after **[d]**) **Organise a full week of prayer and fasting for global revival**

finishing minutes before the next Sunday morning service.

5

Church Music

Ever wondered why friends say they don't understand a thing when they visit your church? Well, at least part of the problem is the hymns—the language of them.

While some modern choruses leave a little to be desired on the old theology front—and repeat themselves endlessly—most churches rely on hymns written hundreds of years ago, in the (then) everyday language.

Unfortunately language changes. More unfortunately, churches usually don't.

Christmas is a classic time for miscommunication. People who wouldn't normally go to church are there imagining heaven to be even duller than church because they are listening to a carol which says 'All in white shall wait around', and have to ponder such classics as 'Rise the woman's conquering seed/Bruise in us the Serpent's head'. What does all this mean? Beats us.

49. Do-it-yourself hymnwriting

There is something you can do to liven things up—try composing a new hymn from the archaic language and ridiculous hymn-speak in your church hymnal. Have a bash with these classic examples of 'hymn-speak':

'To Thy temple I repair'
'awful Father'
'co-eternal'
'bowers'
'heavenly guerdon'
'pavilioned in splendour'
'rending of the veil of clay'
'Let me stand by faith on Heaven's tableland'
'helpless estate'
'flowery beds of ease'
'a mighty bulwark'

'eternal verity'
'consbustantial'
'bedewing'
'divers mansions'
'shining carbuncles'
'sundered wide'
'Come to His house of wine'
'the trump shall resound'
'attendeth my way'
'deck thyself my soul with gladness'

...phew!
Whatever you come up with may not make much sense—but then neither do some of the originals these days.

50. Songs to liven up your services

Revive the musical heritage of the Christian church.

Inane repetition is nothing new in the Christian church. People have slipped into it from the beginning—Jesus even warned us about 'vain repetition'.

These days it is a particular hazard when it comes to popular songs and choruses, but it was also common during the Victorian era. Sadly many of these songs have fallen into disrepair or disrepute. Can't think why.

Why not introduce some into your church for a change if your musical diet is a touch on the snoring side.

Here are some examples—choruses only—from popular songs of the last century. If they weren't anonymous they certainly should have been—and we're certainly not about to give the writers any credit here. Feel free to revive them. Invent your own verses:

> I'm on the pill
> I'm on the pill
> I'm on the pilgrim's way.
>> Anon. (And we know why.)

> I want a man
> I want a man
> I want a mansion in the sky.
>> Anon anon anon....

> Stir the stew
> Stir the stew
> Stir the stupid hearts of men.
>> And on....

51. Changing your tunes

If you think about it, the church as a whole has a long history of stealing other people's tunes.

General Booth, who started the Salvation Army, pinched pop tunes of his day to sing his words to. The Sally Army were getting-on down to the equivalent of Bananarama and Bros long before anyone dreamed up the Performing Rights Society or the concept of Artists' Royalty. Useful that.

*Pastor Morgan's colossal organ drew crowds
from far and near…*

Nowadays of course we know better...er...but still the same thing goes on.

The Sixties was a fertile time for stealing tunes. Everybody got ripped off by trendy and talent-free church composers from The Animals' 'House of the Rising Sun' to the theme tune to the film *The Dam Busters*.

Whose tune will be the next to go? Pick a tune from this list and write your own lyrics to fit the scan. (No need to bother too much about the words fitting—churches never have. Also no need to worry about endless repetition if you can't write enough words, banal rhyme or sheer enthusiasm will carry the day. You see, no-one minds in church because it's all in a good cause. Also no need to pay [or even credit] the owner of the tune—if he or she knew you were using it they would doubtless give their permission...wouldn't they?)

If you want to use any of the songs below for your sacred singing, just get in touch with the artist concerned—they'll be pleased to hear from you.

Don't Stand So Close to Me (stand close to Him)—*Sting*
Money for nothing (and the bread and wine are free)—*Mark Knopfler*
His way—*Frank Sinatra*
Saints in white satin—*Moody Blues*
Karma Communion—*Boy George*
Born again to run—*Bruce Springsteen*
Stand by Him—*Leiber & Stoller*
Good—*Michael Jackson*
Like the Virgin—*Madonna*
All along the clock tower—*Bob Dylan*
God's message in a bottle—*Police*

Every prayer you make — *Sting*
Bohemian rapture — *Queen*
Born again in the USA — *Bruce Springsteen*
Preaching all over the world — *Status Quo*
He loves you, yeah, yeah, yeah — *The Beatles*
He ain't heavy, He's my Father — *The Hollies*
Mistletoe and Communion wine — *Cliff Richard*

Ecclesiastical Dress Sense

God, it seems, has an odd attitude to clothes. The trouble started in The Beginning when he forgot to give Adam and Eve any. Not a stitch.

Well, either he forgot or he liked it that way. Maybe God doesn't wear clothes himself. Interesting theological point.

Anyway, even when Eve and Adam went to the tailor's they only came away with some skimpy little numbers. Ever since then people have insisted on putting on more and more clothes for church— getting further and further away from the original idea.

Odder still, ministers, vicars and pastors wear even more than most of us. That's why they are called 'men of the cloth'.

52. Dressing for church

People who are not brought up in the church often find it very amusing when they see, say on TV, the

It was then that the congregation realised that it was time
for Rev Redneck to move on…

way some people dress up to run their churches—all frilly nighties and curtains with tassles. It wasn't always so funny.

Today's chiffon-clad clergy originally took up ecclesia-fashion—smocks, cassocks, dog-collars, etc—to demonstrate they were no different from the ordinary working man or woman.

They were trying to symbolise what they had recently rediscovered, the 'priesthood of all believers'—ie, the minister wasn't any closer to God because he stood in a pulpit—so they dressed like other teaching classes at fifteenth-century universities.

So, why not persuade your vicar/minister/priest/ deaconess that he or she needs to re-emphasise this important theological truth—that he or she is just an ordinary Joe (or Jo).

Buy a new outfit or two which might symbolise other theological views.

Suggested fashion tips

(a) Joe Cool: buy your minister some jeans, a T-shirt and a pair of shades.

(To demonstrate that he/she is just one of us.)

(b) WC Plumber—put him in workman's overalls and stick his Bible in a toolbox.

(He ought to be a Mister Fixit for his congregation.)

(c) Manuél—give him a bow-tie, stick a tea-towel over his forearm and tell him to take the orders.

(He's here to serve.)

(d) Justice Dunn—fix him up with a judge's wig.

(He ought to be on the side of justice.)

(e) Hosé—put him in a fireman's outfit with bucket and hosepipe.

(The first on the scene in difficult and fiery situations.)

(f) John Peck—dress him in a pantomime hen costume.

(Like Jesus for Jerusalem, your minister would gather his congregation under his wings—like a hen her chicks.)

(g) Paul (dare-to-be-a) Daniels—top hat and magic wand.

(Symbolises God pulling everything out of his hat—creating from nothing.)

*The members of St Adam and Eve's believed in
stripping away unnecessary traditions . . .*

7

Festivals in the Church Year

95 GRIPES

(Continued)

24. More volume during choruses (young people).

25. Less volume during choruses (old people).

26. More pub visitation.

27. A ban on non-alcoholic communion wine.

28. Replace the pews with comfy armchairs.

29. Throw out the old

P.T.O.

For some reason the church loves festivals. Except, unlike everyone else, they have forgotten how to have a party. But fear not, *we* haven't!

Festivals in the church year—some new ones

53a. Teenagers' Sunday

Like Saints' Days but...er...not quite so saintly. It's a day when being a teenager is celebrated—instead of being cursed as it quite often is. All Ancient and Modern Hymns to be replaced by only modern Top Forty material. Teenagers get to wear whatever they like in church, for a change. Mums and Dads have to shut up. What a blessing.

53b. Children's day

All the boring, mature adults get to behave like children for a day. 'Suffer the little children' (and the not-so-little children).

54. Ministering Sunday

Like Mothering Sunday, but different. It's a compulsory day off for your Minister, and therefore a day off for you too. A veritable shower of blessings.

55. Wittenberg door day

This celebrates the day in the sixteenth century when Martin Luther nailed his ninety-five theses to the door of the church in Germany and ushered in the Protestant Reformation.

On this day you also nail your ninety-five gripes to the vestry door—listing what needs to be changed and how you intend to change it—your own reformation. (If you get kicked out of church you are in good company—so did Martin Luther. You can start your own church, as he did.)

Examples:

'We the congregation demand:

(1) Shorter sermons
(2) Better coffee for after-church friendly bit
(3) Better hats for the old ladies
(4) New rock-and-roll hymn book
(5) Less polish on pews to avoid sliding off when sleeping
(6) Fewer books to juggle
(7) Right to reply to silly sermons
(8) Right for women to be equal with men
(9) Right for men to have babies...in church
(10) Music lessons for the organist
(11) Crash diet for the choir
(12) Softer loo paper

(13) Maximum ten screaming babies at one time

(14) Right not to be pressured when the collection plate comes round

(15) Right not to smile

(16) Stewards stop behaving like night club bouncers

(17) Right not to be always fund-raising

(18) Right to have the heating on sometimes

(19) Right to arrive late...sometimes

(20) ...or not at all sometimes

(21) Freedom not to 'go forward' at all altar calls

(22) Permission to have eyes open during prayer

(23) No pressure to pray in 'open prayer time'

(95) Trivial Pewsuit in each pew

Certain saint's days were more popular than others…

Church
Problem
Solving

Have you noticed how there are certain things that go on in your church which, if you changed the context, would seem completely daft anywhere else? So have we.

56 The preacher's dreadful 'preaching voice'

Somewhere, way back in the arcane theological training establishments that turn out men, and now women, for ordination, there is a lengthy and difficult course on 'how to speak in the pulpit'—ie, how to sound completely different when you are preaching from when you are talking normally.

This fascinating science arose hundreds of years ago as a direct result of larger church buildings and lack of amplification. It is said that in order to make oneself heard without going hoarse in a medieval cathedral one had to chant or intone—it helped the

'My theme for today is effective communication...'

voice carry. Sounds reasonable. But that was then and this is now.

Most churches now have decent microphones and amplification. But many preachers still do it probably because they mistakenly think it gives them added authority.

The question is—did Jesus need to put on a funny voice to speak to the crowd? Did he feel that ordinary people would take him more seriously if he sounded as if he was from another planet? Unlikely.

How to cure your preacher

1. The kindest way to help your preacher is to allow him to hear what he sounds like on a tape. It may be that he or she has never heard a recording of their voice in 'preaching mode'. If you can arrange for them to hear the tape 'accidentally', all the better. If this doesn't work, try this...

2. The fairly subtle way is to invite the offending person round to a meal with friends with whom he or she can relax. Afterwards play a game of 'What's My Name'. Prepare in advance a series of tapes of your guests talking normally, then play them to the group and let everyone identify the 'mystery voices'. Not very hard—except that you will have already primed your other guests to feign ignorance of your preacher's identity when his tape is played. Get them to say things like: 'I'm sure I've never met that person'; 'Does anyone really speak like that?' If your subject doesn't take the hint, use this method...

57. 'Evangelicution' lessons

Teach your whole church to speak like your preacher does.

Hint: Instead of pronouncing the word 'yes', say 'ears'. Speak in a slightly sing-song tone three times louder than is natural, as if the person you are speaking to is terribly deaf. *Put* the emphasis *in* your sentences *on* prepositions, and it can help to have a rising inflection on the end of most sentences—this sounds more 'challenging'.

58. The church 'split'

Usually to be found in the aerobics class led by the minister's wife. To be avoided.

59. 'Gifts' or 'no gifts'?

The church for years has been divided over the question of gifts. We say that Birthdays and Christmas are fine...and maybe the occasional anniversary.

60. How to be 'sound'

Just say yes...to whatever the pastor says you should believe.

61. How to be 'unsound'

Make the fatal mistake of not hanging up your brains with the hats and coats when you come into church.
Here are some sure-fire ways to become unsound:

(1) Not believing in a seven-day creation
(2) Not believing in 'the baptism of the Spirit'
(3) Believing in 'the baptism of the Spirit'
(4) Admitting you have smoked
(5) Admitting you have not read the Bible recently
(6) Admitting you don't have a Bible
(7) Owning up to kissing your spouse before marriage

62. How to be 'covered'

Get a hat...for goodness sake.

63. How to be 'uncovered'

Be bold...take it off.

64. How to be excommunicated

The quickest way to be excommunicated is to write a book called *101 Things To Do with a Dull Church*.

9

Responsibilities, Obligations and the Church Rota

Of course, being a church member isn't all fun. It does have its responsibilities. Take hygiene for example.

In The Beginning—church cleaning wasn't a problem. There were no churches.

Jesus—who said he had nowhere to lay his head—invited people to follow him, into the countryside...er...wandering about.

Unfortunately with the coming of institutionalised Christianity—monasteries, convents, churches, etc—people started getting all capitalistic and having their own buildings. Buildings needed looking after. Looking after needed the dreaded 'rota'.

65. Dispensing with the building: the house church option

Simple. You dispense with church cleaning by dispensing with the church building.

You meet in your front room. As long as you don't

become too keen and start to meet every day, you won't need to do any extra cleaning.

WARNING: for some reason House Churches often become 'keen'. Then they start 'being led' to meet in the local school—another cleaning rota—then they start believing they should 'invest in the future of God's work in the area'—ie, build a building that needs cleaning. Be careful.

66. The gift of scrubbing: the faith option

You may have heard over the last ten years of the New Wave of the Holy Spirit leading certain church groups to speak in tongues, to heal the sick, to preach long and often very dull sermons, to raise the dead and sing very loudly. For some reason this new driving force through these churches has not manifested itself greatly in the gifts of church maintenance. Why not ask for these coveted gifts?

The gift of unblocking the ladies' toilets; the gift of pulpit polishing; the gift of getting those pesky pigeons out of the belfry; the gift of floor scrubbing; the gift of cleaning the windows. Why not go further and see if you can pray for them to be done without your involvement at all?

Surely, if faith can move mountains, it can clean the toilets.

67. Running a fellowship group without actually being there
Practical tips:

(a) THE TAPE RECORDING (An old trick—but it still works!)

(b) REMOTE CONTROL: use your *Robovicar* (see No. 44) or your *Walkmin* to take care of the

meeting. Or set up an audio-visual link link from the comfort of your own armchair to the house-group where your fellowship group members await your leadership. Because you can see them but they can't see you—you can have friends round, have a dinner party or watch *Minder* at the same time.

(c) SHOUT VERY LOUDLY: (see Ian Paisley).

(d) TV LINK-UP: like (b) but different—because they can see you too. Has disadvantages—you have to stay awake.

(e) DELEGATION: a common trick in many churches. Simply means if you don't want to lead your house group you get someone else to do it who hasn't got the nerve to refuse—or who thinks that leadership makes you more spiritual. Men often rope women in here.

(f) THE D-I-T KIT (Do-It-Themselves Kit): using

plain paper, clear writing and sharp thinking, write down the various steps that go to making a house group run smoothly:

eg, step: (1) Everybody sit down
(2) The tallest person opens in prayer
(3) The nearest person with glasses says amen after thirty minutes
(4) Anyone with red socks reads the Bible
(5) Discussion: always dominated by extrovert know-alls who lack the gift of listening
(6) Coffee

or　　　proceed instead to number 6

68. Coping with a church council or PCC

This has turned into a resigning issue for so many people that we have decided to write a whole book on the subject to be published in 1998. Sorry to disappoint you.

69. Reading the lesson

Just for the fun of it, why not try to read the lesson as if it were a letter from a friend you had received that very morning?

However, if you find people waking up from their reverie and actually listening to you—you must immediately revert to the traditional monotone delivery otherwise people might think something was wrong.

70. The flower rota

To liven up the proceedings, next time you do the flowers buy a bunch of Venus Flytraps and arrange them where everyone can see them.

*The new Fellowship Group Control System
was a vast improvement*

During the long, dull hours of the Sunday service count the number of flies and bluebottles that get eaten for lunch.

If there happen to be no flies in your church (or on your pastor) bring out a jam jar with previously caught flies and flick them into the mouths of your beautiful flower arrangement.

NOTE: Fly Traps have been known to belch rather loudly having had a good feed.

71. Leading the prayers

Why not replace some of your traditional church prayers with some of those from Chapter 3?

72. After church refreshments

Drop a handful of senna pods into the coffee urn when you are asked to make the refreshments. We guarantee you will never ever be asked to make the coffee again.

*'And a big thank-you to Miss Thrush for
this week's flower display.'*

Advice on
Counselling

The first word of counsel to offer on counselling is 'don't'.

The second is...we can't remember what the second one is...er...yes...you need a good memory. In particular, try to remember your client (ie, the person you are counselling)'s name. It's more sensitive somehow.

73. Principles of good lively counselling

(1) Don't take on counselling when there aren't lots of juicy details. You'll just fall asleep.
(2) That's it.
(3) We said that's it...are you asleep already?

74. Counselling pitfalls
Professional distance

(1) Never, never get 'involved' with your client. In fact some people find the best technique to avoid

involvement is never to meet the client—this is, of course, very effective.

(2) If you do meet your client, however, you can try counselling them on the other side of a door—preferably with them outside your front door—using the letter box or key hole to communicate. You may need to lend them an umbrella.

Members of an opposing sex

(1) If you suspect your client of being a member of an opposing sex to yourself, you may be in trouble. In the past counsellors have often been 'compromised'. No one actually knows what this means, but it sounds frightful, so the best policy—if you do suspect your client of being a member of a different sex from yourself—is to ask them to leave. If you cannot tell what sex they are, or you cannot tell what sex you are, you may have to 'compare bits'—but since this is a family publication which has already been banned in some bookshops around the country, we'll leave that to our next book *101 Ways To Tell Christian Men And Women Apart*. Sorry about that. (Written details are available on request plus £36.50 p&p.)

75. How to make yourself look more impressive

The problem-free counsellor

No one wants to go to someone, pour out all their troubles and hurts, make themselves vulnerable and maybe even start to (horror of horrors, dare we say it) cry—only to find that their counsellor has similar experiences. Can you imagine? It blows all credibility. A favourite trick therefore—especially among the clergy—is to be completely above it all. What the clergyman is doing is creating a wonderful ideal that

Father O'Reilly knew how to steer his flock

you—poor wretch—can aspire to. The trouble is most people fail to see the lives of the clergy as a shining example, for some reason.

This is probably where Jesus went wrong. He should have been more separate from the common people.

76. How to make the client feel stupid and guilty

A favourite technique for counsellors, and easily achieved. You do very little. All you do is snort with derision every time the person who has come for counselling mentions anything sensitive to them.

This is a useful ploy if lunch is on the table and you want to get rid of the client.

WARNING: For some reason, on the odd occasion, counsellors using this technique have been attacked by overwrought clients. Lunch will make you feel better.

77. Affirmation: Barry and Maureen—a case study

The following real-life scene was taken from the case-book of Maureen, who is a trainee Counsellor and Reader at St Wally's, Woking. The client in this instant was Barry, who was standing on a window ledge preparing to jump.

Maureen: Don't do it, Barry! Don't do it, Barry! *(Note use of client's first name.)*
Barry: There's nothing to live for.
Maureen: Barry! There is, Barry! *(Still using first name.)* You're liked—well liked!

Barry:	**No I'm not. My dog hates me, my cat** hates me, my wife hates me—even the Vicar hates me.
Maureen:	It's not that bad.
Barry:	It is! You don't know how bad it is!
Maureen:	But you're throwing your life away.
Barry:	I know. I'm going to j....
Maureen:	Barry, just give me thirty seconds. There must be some hope in your life, somethng you can look to, something you can grasp, something you can hold, something you can embrace, something you can own, something to give you hope, meaning and purpose...a ray of hope however faint, a candle in the darkness, a clearing in the jungle, a light at the end of the tunnel! I mean, which football team do you support?
Barry:	Bolton.
Maureen:	Bolton? Oh.
SFX:	(SPLAT)

Sadly Barry jumped to his death.

But what did Maureen learn from the experience? Didn't she use his first name enough? Did she fail in affirmation? No.

'Bolton Wanderers Supporters are a very particular group, and we would in future refer such cases to a specialist in really terrible football teams.'

78. Empathy: Peter and Maureen (again)—a nutcase study

The following real-life encounter was again taken from Maureen's casebook.

Peter: I'm in a mess.
Maureen: Mmm....
Peter: I feel awful.
Maureen: Mmmmmm....
Peter: Really awful.
Maureen: Mmmmmmmmm....
Peter: Terrible.
Maureen: Mmmmmmmmmmmm....
Peter: Suicidal really.
Maureen: Mmmmmmmmmmmmmmmm....
Peter: Well, I mean, what's left for me?
Maureen: Mmmmmmmmmmmmmmmmm....
Peter: I've got this loaded revolver here in fact.
Maureen: Mmmmmmmmmmmmmmmmm....

Peter's life was in fact saved because at this point he fell asleep. Maureen had cleverly been asleep for at least half the interview. This highlights one of the advantages of empathy—you don't have to be awake.

11

Advertising and Marketing

St.
Matthew's
p.l.c.

Sunday Services 10:30p.m. & 6:30p.m.
Vicar: Rev. Mammon
We accept all major credit cards

Anyone who has even the slightest idea about church knows that a big part of their problem is that they have such a bad image. All this talk of sin and so on doesn't exactly go down a storm with the target audience (ie, people like you and me). So, what needs to be done is to hire a decent advertising agency. If, however, the budget does not stretch to that, no matter, because you can do it yourself very very easily.

Here you will find all you need to know to put the Saatchi brothers out of business.

79. The mail shot

The most effective mail shot seems to be this one:

Dear *Mr and Mrs Uninterested*

You have been selected from thousands of hopeful other people in your area to receive a **fabulous and unique free gift!**

The great computer in the sky has thrown up your

name as someone who would appreciate the spectacular gift of **ETERNAL LIFE!!**

This unique, never to be repeated, once in a lifetime opportunity will be made available to you, *Mr and Mrs Uninterested*, by the Rev Johnnie Flashman at the 6.30 pm Evangelistic Service at St Dismal's this Sunday!!!

Eternal Life: where would you be without it?!!!

(Money back if not completely satisfied in thirty days.)

Yours unctuously

The Rev John Flashman

(Member of the Institute of Practitioners in Advertising)

80. The poster

Put this poster up outside your church:

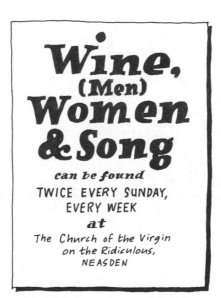

In the parish of St Kilda's, it wasn't just God who moved in mysterious ways...

81. The Radio Commercial

Get the neighbourhood excited about your church by using a catchy jingle on your local commercial radio station. Get the musicians in your church to record this timeless evangelistic ditty to the tune of 'There is a green hill'.

Sung:

> We are St Swithin's not far away
> Within these city walls,
> Where you can hear a powerful word
> About the meaning of it all.

82. The TV commercial

Same as above, but add pictures. (Make sure the pretty young women are at the front.)

83. A high profile in your neighbourhood

One of the few under-exploited advertising opportunities left is to preach your message *from the sky!* Try this:

Invite the Ladies' Sewing Circle to fashion a gigantic hot-air balloon from the choir robes.

Take the pulpit out onto the church lawn and attach it underneath the balloon and get your preacher to stand in the pulpit. Instruct him to start preaching his longest and most hot-air filled sermon. Soon he will have inflated the balloon and be airborne over your town, preaching the message from the clouds.

This ingenious approach, apart from being a danger to birds, also kills a number of them...with one stone...er...balloon. Not only are the local community now hearing the Word From On High, but you have also neatly dispatched the dull choir robes,

the dull pupit, your dull preacher and his dull sermon.
Praise the Lord!

*Deacon Dora's Church Growth studies
soon paid dividends...*

Sacred
Recreational
Pursuits

OK, you have decided not to blame anyone else for the tedium in church—it is time you yourself made church life more interesting. What you need is sacred recreation.

84a. Hang gliding with the vicar's vestments

When you can stand it no longer, tie the Vicar's vestments to your arms and legs (easier if he is not wearing them). Climb onto the highest rafter in the church and fling yourself off on your maiden flight. Award yourself ten points for every pew you fly over. Subtract ten points for every bone you break.

84b. Pumping scripture

Scripture is meant to 'build up the body'. Use the enormous Bible from the lectern for weightlifting—beginners can start with the New Testament. Complete weeds can start with the second letter of John—

*The Bishop had set his heart on a third runway in
the north transept...*

which is the shortest book in the Bible—one page long.

84c. Ballet practice on the altar rail

Practice your pointing and perfect your pirouetting by prancing and posing in your tutu—preferably not during Communion.

84d. Pigeon shooting in the church tower

This has often been used as an evangelistic tool to reach the upper classes before the opening of the grouse season. 'PULL!'

85. Sleeping in the church services

A time-honoured ecclesiastical pastime—passed down through the ages. First established during one of St Paul's longer sermons. Not recommended for seats on balconies or window sills.

86. Camps, conferences, conventions

There are big differences in attitudes towards extra-curricular activities like these. Basically, they break down into three groups:

(1) **The Children's Holiday Camp.** (Camp in the old sense of the word.) Generally at the seaside. Specialise in retaining First World War terminology, eg, Adjutant, Commandant, Quartermaster. Favourite song: 'Onward Christian Soldiers'.

(2) **The Church Conference.** Generally organised by 'keen' churches who are trying to get their members into one place in order to get them to 'do business with God'. (What business do they think He is in?)

Things to avoid: spud bashing, washing up, organising the treasure hunt.

What to go for: offer to look after the kids outside—and sleep off the conference in the sun.

(3) **The Convention.** The convention generally has more of an American or international influence. Big emphasis here on satellite link-ups; taking the world by storm; global evangelism etc. Lots of fighting talk. Not much mention of one's neighbour—but plenty talk nonetheless.

Avoid: anything in holiday camps.

Recommended: exotic foreign locations when the church is footing the bill.

87. The great crusade

Crusades are not nearly as popular within the church as they used to be. No one seems to know why this is. In the middle ages crusades were very easy to organise because the raw materials were very close to hand: blindness; hatred; and selfishness. You just can't beat this combination—unfortunately this approach has undermined the church's reputation ever since.

Today's crusades are very different. They usually involve Billy Graham or one of his disciples. This is what to do:

1. Hire an advertising agency
2. Appeal for a lot of money
3. Double it
4. Declare a 'Century of Evangelism'
5. Get a big choir
6. Check that Cliff can make it
7. Change the dates if he can't
8. Hire several football stadiums

*The man from the Guinness Book of Records was
the first to go forward...*

9. Get on Wogan
10. Get on with it

88. Organise a music and arts festival

This could be a wonderful idea.

Organise as many painters, poets, musicians, writers, plumbers, thinkers, singers, dancers, actors, body builders, bricklayers, furniture makers, mothers, composers, computer buffs, photographers, brain surgeons, film makers, dress makers, cooks, philosophers, administrators, do-ers, be-ers, helpers, hinderers, children, friends, relations, animals, the poor and the rich to arrive to spend the weekend together in a field in the middle of Britain.

Then: swap ideas. Celebrate, commiserate, cogitate, ruminate, masticate. Listen.

Then: dance, cry, sing, laugh, argue and chat.

And then: make plans accordion.

Then: call it Greenbelt.

Fund
Raising

The Apostles Peter and Paul, let alone Jesus, never put 'fund-raising' on the agenda of their meetings.

Strange as it may seem, they funded their activities from a 'common purse'. A very unfashionable idea these days.

Fortunately, the church through the ages has learned from its early naïvety and nowadays embarks on perpetual fund-raising from jumble sales to stocks and shares.

That way it insures against having to rely on the sacrificial giving of its members. Clever, eh?

Fund-raising is easy—if you adopt the right approach. Grabbing the attention of enormous numbers of people is the best approach.

89. Hire a TV evangelist
Or, if that fails...

90. Become a TV evangelist

NB If you have a 'complicated' private life or tendency to hypocrisy, don't bother.

91. Selling out

When the vicar/minister/pastor/lady worker is on holiday, put a FOR SALE sign in front of the church with your own phone number for enquiries. Sell the building to the highest bidder.

Prospective purchasers will include bingo halls, mosques, recording or TV studios and the ones who didn't get the building in your last church split.

92. Letting out.

Make a sign like this:

LARGE UNDER-USED BUILDING AVAILABLE. ANY USES POSSIBLE. ANYTHING CONSIDERED (EXCEPT BORING SERVICES AND DULL SERMONS).

Set yourself up as an ecclesiastical letting agent and advertise your dull church building as a venue for these exciting activities:

(a) A spiritual singles bar.
(b) An indoor Arsenal/Tottenham derby match.
(c) A wet cassock competition for the local clergy—male and female.
(d) Indoor hangliding Olympics.

You may need to halt church services for some of the above, but not for the activity below:

(e) An insomniacs' crisis centre

93. Dress occasions

Put this add in yoour local paper to rent out your minister:

> DO YOU FANCY A FANCY-DRESS PARTY BUT ONLY HAVE A FEW FRIENDS? FULLY DRESSED VICAR IN AUTHENTIC COSTUME—IDEAL FOR BUMPING UP NUMBERS AT PARTIES. RATES NEGOTIABLE. WILL POSE FOR PHOTOS. INCENSE EXTRA. CHOIR AVAILABLE.

94. The prayer letter

Prayer letters have always been sent out in large numbers. And read in small numbers. Usually because they are long and dull. Yours won't be.

Keep it short and simple:

> Dear Praying Fiends (put it down to a typing error)
> Weather is fine...
> Send money now.
> Cheques and credit cards accepted.

95. The jumble sale

The Jumble Sale is a marvellous weapon in the fund-raiser's arsenal. It is only surprising that more churches have not discovered the secret of making big money. It's right there in the Bible.

And that secret is... 'Sell all you have and give it to the poor.'

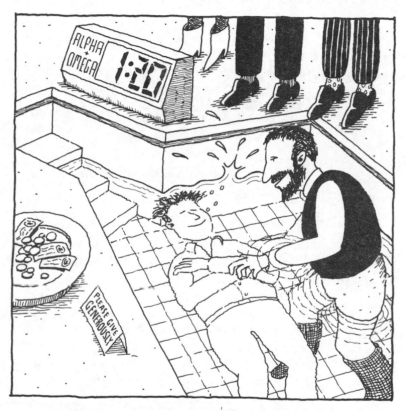

*Undergoing sponsored immersion was Gilbert's
particular ministry...*

96. The whist drive

No one knows what a whist drive is—but it sounds good.

97. The coffee morning

The trouble with the Coffee Morning is that it never sounded exciting—until now. All you have to do is print up some invitations like this:

JOAN COLLINS
INVITES YOU TO COFFEE
AT HER PLACE
(YOUR ADDRESS)
(TIME)
£65 Ensures a place on the sofa
(Bring your own coffee)

98. The fete

The trouble with fetes in Britain is the weather. This is easily solved by holding your church fete while you are on holiday abroad.

You can do one of two things:

(1) Take the fete to Spain with you (though your Spanish may not be up to explaining what a tombola is to the locals). Or:

(2) Make sure the fete happens back home while you are on the beach. Walk around selling tickets to the sunbathers who will think you are a local. Experience shows that nudist beaches are more lucrative because people want to get rid of you.

99. The scandal

A scandal is a great money-spinner.

The tabloid newspapers love to print stores about

sex. However, they will beat a path to your door to buy a story about *religion* and sex, because for some reason they think that God didn't invent sex, or that religious people are all celibate. So what you need is a decent headline like:

VICAR RUNS OFF WITH HIS OWN WIFE! SHOCK! HORROR! PROBE! PHOTOS! EXCLUSIVE!

If you can arrange to borrow your minister's diaries—all the better—they can be serialised in the Sunday papers. It doesn't matter how boring they are because people only read headlines. Any grainy, out-of-focus photos you have will be worth a fortune. (Your old school photos will do nicely.)

Thoughts
for the
Desperate

100. Emergency Services

a. Is there a doctrine in the house?

In the event of extremely dull services one useful fail-safe is to ponder meditatively on some of the great doctrines of the Christian faith: the Creation; the Fall; the Incarnation; the Atonement; the Bodily Resurrection of Jesus; the Holy Spirit and his/her gifts; the Parousia, etc.

A moment or two in quiet perusal should certainly convince you that however mysterious are the ways of God, they are certainly not as dull as the service you are in at the moment.

b. Doctrine on call

Like the above, but a slightly different pun.

c. Young doctrines

This is a new religious drama (soap-opera) in which a clutch of new beliefs (doctrines) come to persuade

Surbiton Presbyterian tended to shun modern translations...

believers that they are the real thing even though they have only been discovered two millennia after the life of Christ.

Popular young doctrines include:

'Health and Wealth' (is the entitlement of all obedient Christians).

'Instant Physical Healing' (from any complaint if you have enough faith).

'Shepherding' (of all Christians by senior ones to make sure they never learn personal responsibility).

'Infallibility of the King James Version' (centres on the idea that an English translation of the Bible dating from the seventeenth century is the one that God himself reads and therefore so should all true Christians).

'Billy Blessing' (to do with the belief held by many conservative British Christians that the only way to get British pews filled up by the British public again is to constantly bring back to the UK an 'elderly imported American' by the name of Billy Graham).

d. Let me through, I'm a doctrine

Always useful, particularly if your Christian experience is based on a warm feeling that left quietly a few days after you 'asked Jesus into your heart'. Always reassuring in a dull service to know that, however dull this church is, it doesn't invalidate the historic truth of Christianity—it's to do with historic facts like the life and death and life of Christ. Not the deathly dull service you are stuck in at this moment.

Rev Pyle took biblical exposition very seriously...

15

Thoughts for the Day

101. Our ministry—what this book is really getting at...

No decent Christian book is complete without a challenge...we all know that...and we hope that you didn't think you'd get away without one in this book.

Maybe we have gone a little too far in some of the things we have said in this book—but that brings us to the interesting subject of our *ministry*.

In fact, many people who have seen this book have actually asked: 'Martin, Adrian, I liked this book. I laughed. It contains essential truths about the church, life the universe and everything...but...but...in the end...at the end of the day...come judgement day...come that great accounting in the heavenlies... *what on earth is your MINISTRY?'*

Well,...er...we're glad you asked that...there are a number of possible answers here and we will take them one at a time...

Our ministry. Our *ministry. Our ministry.*

Is it the Ministry of Defence perhaps? Or the Ministry of Funny Walks, even? The Ministry of Works? Could it possibly be the Ministry of making money? Not with the rotten percentage we're on from Monarch, no. We have our eyes set on higher things...like...like...

But nay, halt, stop, whoa, tarry a tick...gentle reader, are *you* not the real purpose of a book like this? Has it not ministered to you? It has to us...

But perhaps this book hasn't been able to help you with your particular problems. Perhaps you have terrible dress sense; perhaps you are very short; or have chronic dandruff? Don't you think we suffer from these things too? Well since you ask, no, we don't. Martin has a toupee and Adrian is completely bald.

But just because we are servants at the Ministry of Mirth, mere authors who are prepared to be 'fools for Christ', that doesn't make us superhuman, you know...we've got problems too. Why, just the other day Martin got a parking ticket—and the Lord found him the space, too—and Adrian's milk went off in the fridge—can you believe it? Frightening to think these kinds of things can happen in this day and age.

Where were we? Oh, yes...so, your minister preaches three-hour sermons; the organist's wife has got bad breath and insists on kissing you every Sunday; they always use Ribena instead of communion wine? Stop complaining, you can always leave...

But if leaving your church sounds like the easy, worldly way out...then this book has clearly exercised its ministry in your life...and it was well worth the £2.99. Honestly, is this too much to pay to save even one dull soul from a dull damnation?...suddenly, it has become a heaven-sent tool to enable you to face another day, maybe even to save you... from yet another dull church service.

Well, that about covers the ministry... for this book.

101 Things To Do During A Dull Sermon

by Tim Sims & Dan Pegoda

Sermons are great...most of the time. But when your minister has a bad day, and the minutes grind by, surviving to the last 'and finally' can be a tough business. Here are 101 wonderful exercises to keep boredom at bay.

For example:

- Pass a note to the organist asking whether he or she plays requests.
- See if a yawn is really contagious.
- Slap your neighbour. See if he or she turns the other cheek. If not, raise your hand and tell the pastor.
- Try to guess what the sidesmen are doing in the vestry.
- Devise ways of climbing into the balcony without using the stairs.

Author **TIM SIMS** has been chaplain of Death Valley National Park, and now holds a dull job in a dull university. Illustrator **DAN PEGODA** began drawing on church pews at the age of three. He is now art director of *The Wittenburg Door*.

Minstrel
Monarch Publications

All Preachers Great & Small

by Peter Gammons

'A man from Leicester took his grandson to church for the first time. The lad was surprised when the collection plate came round. "You don't have to pay for me, Grandad," he whispered. "I'm not five yet."'

Many have associated religion with a serious disposition and long faces. Peter Gammons sees another side to faith. Here is a hysterical clerical collection of strange facts, stranger anecdotes and shaggy dog-collar stories: bright and sparkling, with a wry, dry twist.

Peter Gammons solemnly swears that, to the best of his knowledge, all the entries in this book are true.

'Farmer seeks lady with tractor with view to companionship and possible marriage. Send picture of tractor.'

Minstrel
Monarch Publications